# SPECTRES OF EXILE

**SPECTRES OF EXILE**
and Other Poems

Hasan Abdallah al-Qurashi

Translated from the Arabic
by John Heath-Stubbs
and Catherine Cobham

**Echoes**

**British Library Cataloguing in Publication Data**

al-Qurashi, Abdullah
   Spectres of exile and other poems: a bilingual
   anthology
   1. Saudi Arabia.Arabic poetry
   I. Title II. Heath-Stubbs, John 1918-
   III. Cobham, Catherine
   892.716

   ISBN 1-873395-36-1
          1-873395−05−1 pbk

First published 1991 by
Echoes, 26 Westbourne Grove
London W2 5RH

Printed in Great Britain by
Billing & Sons Ltd, Worcester

# Contents

# Foreword

Hasan Abdallah al-Qurashi was born in Mecca in 1926 and read history at the University of Riyadh (now King Saud University). He held several posts in the Ministry of Finance, worked in broadcasting and was seconded to the Egyptian broadcasting service for a year. Latterly he has held various diplomatic posts including for a time that of his country's ambassador to Sudan.

He is one of the leading Saudi poets of his generation and his work has been published in the press and in journals as diverse as *al-Ādāb* and *al-ʿArabī*. His first collection of poems came out in 1949 and since then he has had another fourteen volumes of poetry published as well as essays, critical studies and short stories. His works have been translated into French, English, Spanish, Italian and Chinese, and he has represented his country at numerous literary conferences and festivals all over the world.

Al-Qurashi writes love poems in which the pain and difficulty of love are invariably portrayed through imagery relating to the natural hazards of the desert and the nomadic way of life, in keeping with the conventions of his literary forebears:

Your wandering camel-litter bumps and sways across
  the desert

our evening refuge has gone
and the jasmine droops wearily

He also writes about the fate of a poet who is a spokesman for his people and an indivisible part of them, but at the same time an outcast, an exile and a marginal figure. He evokes the beauty of the country to whose past and future he feels bound, but condemns the perversion of its supposedly cherished values and aspirations:

Don't say, 'Tomorrow I will dream dreams'
Your dreams are covered in dust
destroyed by stones and raging sand
You have no kin to support you and the walls have all
    tumbled down

The Hijaz is well known as the birthplace of Arabic poetry and al-Qurashi is inevitably linked by his fellow poets to the great Hijazi poets of the pre-Islamic period and the seventh and eighth centuries AD. 'When I read al-Qurashi, I read…Ibn Abi Rabi'a,' writes the Syrian poet Adonis. 'Umar Ibn Abi Rabi'a (AD 644–712 or 721) was a hero of the milieux of singers and musicians in and around Mecca and a composer of spontaneous lyrical love poetry. In those days the seasons of pilgrimage to the Hijaz were also seasons of poetry, and returning pilgrims carried the poems they heard in and around the holy city all over the Muslim world.

When the Egyptian writer and man of letters Ṭaha Ḥusain heard al-Qurashi reading his poetry in Saudi Arabia in the 1950s he recognized him as an important figure in the rebirth of Hijazi poetry in modern times. A year later he wrote the preface to al-Qurashi's third collection of poetry, introducing the poet to a wider readership and pointing out the influence of modern Egyptian poetry on his work. Ṭaha Ḥusain writes that 'a newness and ease in the language [of al-Qurashi's poetry] make it accessible... at the same time a touch of the calm wisdom of the desert in it is reminiscent of [earlier] Hijazi poetry'. It also resembles this earlier poetry, Ṭaha Ḥusain claims, in the way in which it is 'on the point of depicting the realities of things and calling things by their names, then draws back and chooses to use symbol and allusion instead'.

It would be disingenuous to characterize al-Qurashi's poetry as merely evoking the glorious literary past. The poet's anguish of spirit, his discontent with the hypocrisy, injustice, brutality and corruption around him, his despair as a poet in exile, are entirely contemporary in their expression and he has had to travel further, physically and mentally, than his poetical ancestors. As the Egyptian poet Ṣalāḥ 'Abd al-Sabūr writes, 'Al-Qurashi is not content with the society in which he lives so he criticizes and condemns it...but his protest is invariably poetic and pure.'

*Catherine Cobham*

# ارتهان الحصان

تَساءلتُ فيمَ آرتهنتُمْ حِصاني؟
سلبْتُمْ عِنْانَ الحِصانِ
وسرّجَ الحِصانَ
وسمّرتُموا برصاصِ الخيانةِ حافِرَهُ في الطّريقِ؟
وأجبرتُموني على السيرِ في جَمرَة القيظِ وحْدي
أخوّضُ في المنحدَرْ
حنانيكمُو
أنا ما كنتُ يوماً ولا ساعةً
واحداً من رُعاةِ البَقَرْ
ولم أحترفْ مرّةً أن أخبّىءَ ظلّي
وراءَ الشجَرْ!
وأندسَّ تحتَ ستارِ المَطَرْ
حنانيكمُو
أنا ما كنتُ لصّاً لقافلةٍ
غادراً بالرفيقْ
،لا سارقاً حفنةً من قَطيعٍ

10

## The Pawning of the Horse

Why did you pawn my horse
steal its reins
and its saddle
stop it in its tracks with the bullets of treason
and force me to walk alone in the burning heat
slipping on the steep road?
I beg your mercy
I was never in my life a herdsman
I never made a practice of hiding my shadow
behind trees
or creeping in under a curtain of rain
I beg your mercy
I have never robbed caravans
betrayed my companions
rustled cattle

ولا قاطعاً للطّريق
ولا مُعْجَباً بلصوص البشرْ!

* * *

وكنتُ بريئاً
فها أنتمُ هؤلاءِ
تبيعونَني
رهْنَ مَذْبح غَدْر المرابينَ والمستبدِّين والأدْعياءِ
شققتُم قميصيَ. . .
جرَّحتُم الحُلُمَ الغَضَّ
حطَّمتُموكلَّ سهْمٍ حَوَاه وفَاضِي
فها هي ذِي جُعْبَتي
أفرغُ اليومَ من ظُلَّة العَنْكَبُوتْ!

* * *

برغمِ الحِصارْ
برغمِ انحسارِ المَدى وانتحارِ النّهارْ
برغم ارتهان حصَاني

12

or held up travellers
I have never admired the thieves among my fellow men

* * *

I was innocent
yet you pawned me at the treacherous altar of
    moneylenders, tyrants and hypocrites
You ripped my shirt
wounded my youthful dreams
broke all my arrows
so now my quiver is emptier than a spider's web

* * *

Despite the siege
despite the vanishing horizon, the day's suicide
despite the pawning of my horse

ساقيَ أنَا

أحاولُ أن أستردَّ السَّنَا

ولكنّني عُذْتُ أرجوكمُو

أن تعيدُوا إليَّ حِصاني

وسَرْجَ حِصاني

وخلَّوا لديكُم عِنَاني

إذا شئتمُوا أن تَغلُّوا زَماني

ولا تحذَرُوا

فارسُ الأمْس

لمَّا يَعُدْ مثلِما كانَ

لمَّا يَعدْ جمرةَ المِهرجانْ

عادَ حُطاماً كَما شئتموه

لقىً في الدُّروبْ

وَهى عَزْمُهُ، وخَبا بَصَراً ثاقباً

وذَوى عودُهُ

فارسُ الأمس

ماذا تخافُونَ من حُزمةِ الحُزْنِ؟

من كُتلةِ الشَّوكِ؟

مِنْ وَمْضةٍ في المَغِيبْ؟!

I shall go on seeking to restore the splendour of the light

But still I would beg you

to give back my horse

and its saddle

Hold on to the reins

if you want to tie me down

And do not fear

Yesterday's rider is not the man he was

He's no longer the leading light of the festival

but a wreck, just as you wished him to be

a piece of dung at your feet

His resolve has weakened

his sharp gaze is dulled

his strength has faded

yesterday's rider

What have you to fear from a bundle of grief

from a bushel of thorns

from a faint gleam in the dying light?

# عندما تتقصف الخيام

برادِيكِ أقطعُ كلَّ الفيافي
وأمشي على دَرَبْ كلِّ الصواعقِ، كلِّ الرعود
خَبرتُ المَنافي
كم احتضنتْي البراكينُ
كم جرَّبتْني العواصفُ
كم هَدْ هَدتْ قَدَميَّ القيود
حجازيةَ الدمعِ
يا ريحَ أشرعتي أنتِ
يا فجوةً للزلازلِ ترتطِمُ الرُّوحُ فيها
وتجري نثاراتِ حبٍّ عنيد!

*\*\**

كأمسِ انتفضْنا معاً
ثم ذُبنا معاً في مَسارِ القوافلِ
في عَصَبِ الريحِ
في تَمتَماتِ ظلالِ الخريفْ
وأيقنتُ أني جسرٌ من الحُزْن

## When the Tents Come Down

To reach your valley I would cross all the deserts
and walk on the paths of the thunderstorms
I have known exile
volcanoes have engulfed me
tempests tried me
and fetters caressed my feet
You cry the tears of the Hijaz
You are the wind that fills my sails
the crack that opens as the earth shakes
and my soul plunges downwards
and stubborn love bursts forth

\* \* \*

Yesterday we trembled together
then melted into the caravan trail
into the sinews of the wind
into the murmur of the autumn shadows
I knew then that I was a bridge of sorrow

لن تقطعَ الجسرَ

لن تركبَ الموجَ

من أرهقتْها الرُّؤى والطُّيوف؟

حذارِ!.. هتفتُ

وأشفقتُ.. في الفم مِلْحٌ

وفي الصدر شوكٌ

وطَرْفي رَمادْ

وأنت تسيرين يرهقك الأيْنُ

والطيبُ منسكبُ الفَوْحِ، يغمرُ وجهَ الوِهادْ

حجازيَّةَ الشوقِ

تذبحني هفةٌ في المحيَّا

ويفجؤني نبضُ نَهْدٍ لَعوبٍ

وَيلجمني السرُّ والذكرياتْ!


\*\*\*


وأبصرتُ كلَّ الخيام عَطَاشى

ملاعبُ خيل الزَّمان تبدَّت لعيني طُلولاً

وأوديةُ الخِصْب قفراً كئيباً

وهودجُكِ الشاردُ المترنِّحُ يلطمهُ التيه

She will never cross the bridge
she will never ride the waves
she whom visions and phantoms weary
'Beware!' I cried
and felt a surge of pity
There was salt in my mouth
there were thorns in my breast
and ashes in my eyes
and you, you walk, weighed down by sorrow
your perfume drifting over the ravines
you yearn the yearning of the Hijaz
the look of longing in your face pierces my heart
I am struck with wonder by the throbbing of your
    lively breast
and made speechless by the secret memories we share

\* \* \*

I saw all the tents were dry and bleached and thirsty
the places where the horses once grazed were deserted
the valleys of plenty were bleak and desolate
Your wandering camel-litter bumps and
    sways across the desert

ولا موئلٌ للعشيّاتِ
والياسمينُ مدلّىً حَسير

***

حجازيةَ الومضةِ المستبدّة
أطيافُك الغُرُّ نَهرٌ من العطرِ
مَزرعةٌ للدوالي
تلالٌ من الصَّندلِ المشرئبِّ
مجامِرُ للمندلِ الرَّطب
آنيةُ الأقحوانِ الفَريد!

***

حجازيةَ الهمسِ بُحَّ الصَّدى في مَسار النجومْ
وَيَجرحُ ليلَ دَوْماً نداكَ مُعَنّى
وينطفىءُ النَّغمِ الحُلْوُ ثمَّ تلوحينَ في ردهاتِ الأسى
تُطعمينَ جراحيَ نُوراً، وناراً
عشقتُك والكونُ ما زالَ طِفْلًا
وشبّابةُ القَلْبِ سَكرَى انتصارِ

our evening refuge has gone
and the jasmine droops wearily

* * *

In the captivating gleam of your eyes you are Hijazi
In my beautiful visions you are a river of perfume
a field of red grapes
a hillside of proud sandalwood trees
a censer for sweet tender wood
a vase for the peerless chrysanthemum

* * *

You whisper in the voice of the Hijaz
it echoes hoarsely in the path of the stars
your anguished call is a wound piercing my night
and the sweet melody dies. Then you appear
    in the halls of sorrow
feeding my wounds with light and fire
I loved you when the universe was still a child
and the heart's flute drunk with triumph

ورنَّحني العِشْقُ، والقَلبُ أعشى ضَرِير

فَمَن أنتِ؟ مَن أنتِ؟

فيم تَلو حينَ في خاطِري كلَّ حينٍ

ففي مُلتَقى الفجر أنتِ

وفي ثَبَجِ البحرِ جَوْهرتي

وعلى مَرْفَأِ الشمسِ شَمْسٌ تُريقُ الضِّياءِ

وأنّى التَفَتُّ أراكِ

أرَى زَهرةَ الياسمينْ!

* * *

حجازيةَ الدمعِ

أخضرُ دمعُكِ

يَنسابُ في رئتي . . يستبدُّ هُهائاً

ويفرشُ كالظِّلِّ أهدابَه

يتوغَّلُ في خاطِري لَهَباً أحمراً

وسراباً بديدْ

لِماذا تَفرُّ طيورُ المُنى من حَديقتنا؟

يَستحيلُ الهديلُ نعيباً؟

لِماذا يرافِقُنا شَجَرُ القحطِ والمَحْل

Love made me dizzy, blinded my heart
Who are you? Who are you?
Why do you appear in my thoughts at each instant?
You are there where day and night meet
my jewel in the depths of the sea
and on the edge of the sun you come to land
a second sun spilling beams of light
I see you wherever I turn
my jasmine flower

\* \* \*

You cry the tears of the Hijaz
they are fresh tears
they flow into my lungs, take over my
    wild breathing
and cover your eyelashes like a veil
They spread through my mind, like a red flame
    or a mirage
Why do the birds of desire fly from our garden?
Why does the cooing of doves turn to the
    croaking of ravens?
Why do trees of barrenness and drought

.في كلِّ دربٍ؟
وينزرعُ الشوكُ في أرض غابتنا وحدَها؟
وتزارُ كلُّ وحوشِ الفَلاةِ بأسماعِنا
لماذا نخافُ؟ نذلُّ؟ نضيعُ؟
وفي كفِّنا سيفُه (ابن الوليد)؟!

24

grow by every road we travel

and our forests bear only thorns?

In our ears all the beasts of the wilderness roar

Why are we afraid, abject, lost

when the sword of courage* is in our grasp?

---

* In Arabic: 'His sword — Ibn al-Walid'. This refers to an early Muslim hero, Khalid Ibn al-Walid (7th century AD) from the Prophet's tribe in the Hijaz, who was known as 'the sword of Allah'.

# كنت لي

قد تحجَّرتُ فالتمسِي النارَ
في غَيرِ قلبي
ولا تَغرقي في شُعاع النجومِ
ولا تَسألي لِمَ قلبي تحجَّر
من بعدِ أن كانَ يرقُصُ
فوقَ حدائقِ شمسِ النهارْ؟

. . .

كان قلبي السؤالَ
وكنتِ إجابةَ هذا السؤال
وكنتِ المحبَّةَ
فانغلقتْ رؤيةُ الحُبّ
وآنطفأت في خضمّ المسافاتِ
في صمتِ كلّ الجنائز
أجنحةُ الوردِ، والياسمين!

. . .

## You Were Mine

I've turned to stone, so seek for fire
in another heart
Don't drown in starshine
Don't ask why my heart is stone
when it used to dance
in the gardens of the sun

* * *

My heart was the question
and you were the answer
you were love
but now the vision of love is blotted out
the whirling petals of rose and jasmine lost
in the yawning oceans of distance
and the silence of funerals

* * *

كنتِ لي . . . كنتِ . . . \
لكنَّ أذرعةَ الغيبِ حين اختبأت
وحينَ تراكَض في شفَق الحُلم ظلُّكِ
وانجابَ ظلِّي . . .
وحينَ تغرَّبتِ فوقَ شواهِدِ كلِّ المقابرِ
قد عُدتِ وَهْماً
حقيقتُه انطمستَ وتعرَّتْ
فأصبحتِ مطمورةَ الهَمْسِ
غائبةً في مَدار السِّنينْ!

***

لم أعدْ ذلكَ المشفقُ المتأنِّي
فتحتَ القباب
أرى النهرَ مستخذياً
وأحسُّك أبعدَ . . . أبعدَ
راجفةً كَد بيب النِّمالِ
كمَجمرةٍ عُبِّثَتْ بالرماد
فلا فَوْحَ تنشُرُهُ
لا شُعاعاً

You were mine, you were mine
but you hid in the arms of the unknown
your shadow raced in the twilight of a dream
and mine pursued it
and roamed in exile over graveyards
You became an illusion
unclear, divested of reality
a subterranean whisper
lost in the circling of years

\* \* \*


I am no longer a man of forbearance
for under the sky's arch
I see the river flow on, obediently
and I feel you further and further away
tremulous like a swarm of ants
like an incense-burner full of ashes
with no fragrance
no fire glowing

سِوى قَبضةٍ من هَبَاءٍ
وذَّراتِ سَجَّنَى التَّوابيتِ
ساقطةً من حُطامٍ مَهينْ . . . !

nothing but a handful of emptiness
coffin dust
dropping from a heap of rubble

# شاطئ الضياع

أعيش في تمزقي أنا أعيش
كنخلةٍ عاريةٍ من اللِّحاءَ والثَّمر
كنجمةٍ حائرةٍ بين قَناديلِ السماءَ
ترقُب أشباحَ الفضاءَ
أتوه بين آلافِ الوجوهِ الكالحاتِ الضائعاتْ
في زحمةٍ من القدر
أحملُ أوزارَ السنين
مرنَّح الخطو معذَّبَ الجبين
يهدُّني التجوالُ في مساربِ الكهوفْ
وخبزيَ الدموعُ كلَّ خبزيَ الدموع
ذخيرتي النشيدُ في مَتاهةِ الحياة
وأَحَيرَة النشيدِ في شواطيءِ الضِّياع
في غَابةِ الغِربانِ في مسيرةِ السأم !


\*\*\*


أحِس حين تجدِبُ الحُقول
وتستحمُّ في جزيرة العدمْ

32

## The Shore of Loss

I live torn apart, I live
like a palm tree stripped of its fruit and bark
like a star straying among the lamps of heaven
gazing upon the phantoms of space
I wander among the thousands of sorrowful faces lost
in the crush of fate
I bear the burdens of years
I sway, my brow furrowed with pain
exhausted by wandering in underground caves
Tears are my daily bread
My supplies a song in the wasteland of life
How confused is the song on the shores of loss
in the forest of carrion birds, on the road of tedium

* * *

When the fields are barren
and winter locusts bathe in the island of nothingness

جنادبُ الشتاء
أحسُّ أني طائر ممزقُ الجَناح
يغلُّه الضبابُ والدّخان
يَسحقُهُ القُنوط
أخافُ لطمةَ الفَراش
أفزعُ حتى من تصارعِ النّمالْ
أحسُّ أني كَائنٌ هَباء
تَلهُّفُ أنا يطلُّ في الظُّنون
وفي دبيبِ الذكريات!

\*\*\*

وفي المساء
وحين يورقُ الأملْ
وتذبُلُ العُيون
يُمرُّ بي خيالها الكسير خَلْفَ ألفِ بابْ
غُصناً من العَذَاب
وَيسخُر الصّحابْ
من وجديَ العقيمِ من خُطى الفقيرِ للسَّرابْ
يمرُّ بي خيالها فينتشي الخَفُوق

34

I feel I am a bird with broken wings

chained down by fog and smoke

crushed by despair

Even the moth that brushes my face is like a blow

the combat of ants terrifies me

I feel I am a man of dust

Steeped in regret I survey my thoughts

and the flow of memories

* * *

In the evening

when hope blossoms

and eyes grow vague with slumber

her sad ghost passes through a thousand doors

a branch of suffering

and my friends mock

at my sterile passion, at my poor drawing of the mirage

her sad ghost passes and my heartbeats race, delirious

في، جَنيَ المزروع بالمُدَى وبالحِراب
يشدُّني خيالُها لعالمِ السَّديمْ
فأجتني الكرومْ
لكنني أضلُّ في حديقةِ النهار
وَيسخر القطارُ من ذَخيرةِ الدُّموعْ!

in my side sown with knives and spears
Her ghost binds me to a hazy world
where I pluck fruits from laden vines
But I lose my way in daylight's garden
The hooting of the train mocks my tears

# غادتي شهرزاد

مَن رأى (شهرزادْ)؟
في القطيفِ المحبَّر ترفُلُ
في صرخةِ الطيب، في خفَقاتِ الفُؤاد
كاشتعالِ مَدَى الفجر، كالنغمِ البِكْرِ
كالحُلّم بعدَ السُّهاد
إيه يا (شَهرزاد)
قُدتِ كلَّ قوافل عُمْرِ الهَوَى
في عصور المحبِّينَ
في دَفَقاتِ الينابيعِ
نَشوى من اَلزَّهو
مغمورةً بالوِدادْ


***


إرجِعي (شهرزادْ)
إرجِعي فالحُدَاه القديمُ تَعالَى
وظلَّ المساء تَمدَّدَ
وأنهارَ فوق أريكته (شهريار)

38

## My Girl Shehrezade

Who's seen Shehrezade
trailing her fine velvet
heralded by the shout of her perfume,
　the fluttering of hearts
like the flaring of dawn, like a virgin melody
like a dream after a sleepless night?
O Shehrezade!
You led the caravans of the age of passion
when the world was full of lovers
among gushing fountains
drunk with flowers
encircled by love

*　*　*

Return, Shehrezade!
Return, for the old chant rises
and the evening shadows lengthen
and Shahrayar has fallen back on the cushions

عادَ طفلًا بريئاً
يخوِّضُ في النهر حرّاً
ويلتحفُ الانكسارْ
سَيفُهُ لم يعدْ مصلتاً مُشهراً يتحدَّى
صدورَ الصبايا الصغارْ
سيفُه عاد مَن خُشَب الوردِ
في ذلةِ الاحتضارْ
أغمدَ السيفَ منكسراً ومَشى حاسرَ الرأسِ
يبكي، ويمرحُ
يُسقِطُ حتى بقايا الإزارْ

***

قد تولى النهار
إرجعي هي ذى الأرضُ ممطورةً
ونسيمُ الزهورِ تماوجَ
في رَدَ هَاتِ الأمل
والقَماري تلحِّن ـ ثمةَ ـ سَكرَى
فنونَ الغَزَلْ
إيه قصّيِّ علينا حديثَك،

become like an innocent child,

playing in the river

He embraces defeat

no more is his sword unsheathed, threatening

the breasts of young girls

It is made of rosewood these days

In the helplessness of dying

he has sheathed it dejectedly and walks bare-headed

now weeping, now playful

letting his loincloth fall

* * *

The day is over

Return, the earth is moist with rain

and the breath of flowers blows softly

in the corridors of hope

Drunkenly turtledoves sing

a medley of love songs

Ah! Tell us your stories

.واسترسلي، جُنَّ فينا السَّأم

قد سُقينا المراراتِ في كُلّ كأسٍ

وُشلَّت أحاسيسُنا ـ في دروبِ الأفاعي ـ مروّعةً ـ

وشَجَانا الندم


\*\*\*


إيهِ يا (شَهرزاد)

هل تناءى المَعَاد؟

وانطوتْ دورةٌ من لَيالي الحَصاد

هل سَرَى العقمُ فينا؟

وسرُّ الخصوبةِ هل عادَ جذْباً وَمحْلا؟

والجَنى عاد ظلًّا؟

(شهرزادُ) اسرعي

في (الرياض) التَقيْنا

وكم يَستبي القلبَ زهرُ (الرياض)

وَمشَى الدفءُ في خَافقَينا نديا

يخدِّر ليلَ السهادْ

إيه يا خبزَ أمسي

وآنيةَ الزهرِ في رحلةِ العمرِ ـ منطوياً ـ

.

42

and let them flow, we have grown bored

we have been given a bitter cup to drink

our senses are crippled with fear on pathways

   where snakes lie in wait

and remorse has saddened us

* * *

Ah Shehrezade!

Why wait so long to return?

Has the cycle of fruitful nights gone by for ever?

Has barrenness spread amongst us

and the magic of fertility turned to drought and famine?

Do the fruit trees merely give shade?

Hurry, Shehrezade

It was in Riyadh we met

a city whose flowers so beguile the heart

that warmth flowed in our breasts like dew

filling the night of wakefulness with langour

O bread of my yesterdays

my hidden vase of flowers on life's journey

وعذابي الجَميل

لم يُعد لي خليلْ

لم يُعد لي مَقيلْ

لم يُعد غيرُ مأواكِ

لا تفجَعي فَرَح القلبِ والروحِ

لا تَسخري بالعليلْ

شَمَت الكلُّ فينا

وأضَحَى الخليلُ لَنا الخُصْمَ

فلْتسرعي (شهرزادْ)

هل تناءى المَعَادْ؟

إنني أنتظِرْ

غادتي (شهرزاد)!

and my sweet torment

I have no dear friend now

no resting-place

You are my only refuge

Do not deprive me of my soul's joy

or make fun of a sick man

Others have gloated over our pain

and our friends have become our adversaries

So hurry, Shehrezade

Why wait so long to return

when I am here, expecting you?

My girl Shehrezade

# مهاجران الى القمر

وحينَ أقلعَ النهارْ
وعدتِ يا صديقتي كدرَّة المَحَار
وحينَ أورقَ السهَر
ورنَّحت أقدامَنا نَداوةُ المَطَر
حسبتُ أنا طائرانِ هاربانِ من قَساوةِ البشر
مهاجرانِ للقَمر
ليلتهَا ما كأَنَ أجملَ القَمَر
ما كانَ أعذبَ الهديلَ في السَّحَر

\*\*\*

وحينَ أقلعَ النهارْ
نسيتُ يا صديقتي . . أني نسيتُ الانتظارْ
وعادَ جُرحي في انهمار
يسأل عنكِ . . . نجمةً مهزومةَ الضياء
أضلَّها الفَضَاءْ
كما أضلَّ روحي في المَساء الانتظارْ

\*\*\*

46

## Two Emigrants to the Moon

When the day was done
and you, my friend, were like a pearl
when the night burgeoned
and we grew drunk on the rain's moistness
I thought of us as two birds fleeing from
    the cruelty of man
two emigrants to the moon
That night, how lovely the moon was!
How sweet the doves' murmuring at dawn!

\* \* \*

When the day was done
I did not remember, my friend, that I'd
    forgotten how to wait
My wound opened afresh
and asked about you – a faint star lost in space
just as my waiting soul was adrift in the night

\* \* \*

حبيبتي . .

رأيتُ في الحُلم الغريب أنا ضائعانْ

طفلان ضائعانِ متعبان

عاشا معاً مشردَينِ في القفار

وقبلَ مولد النَّهارْ

رأيتُ أنا قَد كَبِرنَا قد تزوجنْا وأنجْبنا صغَارْ

وعيشُنا قد كان في مدينةٍ بلا بَشَر

كانَ هناك الصخُر قد كانَ الدخانْ

يغلِّف الآفاقَ . . قد كانَ المطرْ

يلقِّح الأشجارَ لكن لا ثَمَر

أضربتِ الأشجارُ، عربدَ الزَّهرْ

فرحتُ اذ رأيتُ طفلَنا الكبيرَ يعشقُ الخَطَر

قد كانَ يجري كالرِّجال لا يبالي المنحدَر

حصانُه الصغيرُ صاهلٌ ضَجِر

كأن يسيرُ تائهاً لغير ما مَقر

وفجأة ترنَّح الطفلُ . . . وضاعَ في الحُفَر

فزعتُ اذ رأيتُ طفليَ انحسر

كباقةٍ من الورودِ تَنتَثِر

واستيقظَ الحُلُم . . وعادَني السَّهَر

Beloved
I saw in a strange dream that we were lost
two weary children
wandering in the wilderness
and before the birth of day
I saw that we had grown up and married,
    and had children of our own
We lived in a deserted city
where there were only rocks and smoke
as far as the eye could see, and the rain
soaked the trees, but they bore no fruit
they withheld their labour, and the flowers ran wild
I rejoiced to see our eldest child in love
    with adventure
He would race like men do, heedless
    of the precipice
his young horse whinnying in protest
He would stray from the path on to uneven ground
and one day he stumbled and was lost in the ravine
In terror I watched him disappear
like a bouquet of roses scattered in the wind
The dream broke and sleeplessness returned

لكنني أسفتُ يا حبيبَتي
أسفتُ إذ بدا زَواجُنا أُقصوصةً لم تَنتصِر
حكايةً عذراءَ من صُنْع القَمَر!

***

حبيبتي حتّى القَمَر
قد عادَ شوكاً وضباباً وركاماً وحَجَر
أسطورةً بالذكرياتِ تَأْتمر
ويْح البَشَر
حتى القَمَر
ملاذُنا الخصيبُ .. مرآةُ النَّهَر
قد ضيَّعوه فانكسر
حبيبتي لا تحزني .. فلن يُضيعَ بدرَنا جيشُ التَّتر
ففي خيالنا البدورُ تَنتظر
سنُرجعُ البدرَ إذا البدرُ انتحر!

I'm sorry, my love
that our marriage appeared as a story of failure
a virgin tale spun by the moon

* * *


Beloved, even the moon
is now thorns, fog and rubble
a myth concocted by memory
Woe to mankind!
They have lost even the moon
our abundant refuge, the river's mirror
and it is broken in pieces
Beloved, do not grieve
Even the Tartar armies will not destroy our moon
If it kills itself we'll bring it back
for in our imagination there are many moons

# زخارف فوق أطلال عصر المجون

سماويةٌ أنتِ عُلويةٌ
فوقَ أرضٍ من الطين، والحقدِ، والعهرِ
تُرعشها خيلُ كلّ المرابينَ
فوق مَناراتِ عصرِ المُجونْ!

\*\*\*

وقلبيَ التُّرابيَّ تحصدهُ أذرُع النارِ في هَيكلِ القحطِ
تخذُله ذَهلةُ الحُلْمِ
يرفضُهُ شجرُ الوَردِ والياسمين!

\*\*\*

سماويةٌ والثرى مُخصبٌ بالمَهاناتِ
ممتزجٌ بأنين الثكالَى الغريقاتِ
والكونُ منفى اَلحُثّالاتِ
مُهترىءْ

## Flourishes on the Ruins of an Age of Debauchery

Celestial you are, ethereal
in a land of mud, hate and fornication
shaken by the trampling of money-lenders' horses
over the minarets of the age of debauchery

* * *

My earth-bound heart is gathered up by arms of fire
in the temple of sterility
betrayed by the confusion of a dream
rejected by the rose and the jasmine

* * *

You are heavenly, but the earth is rich in shame
mixed with the wailing of bereaved mothers,
    engulfed in sorrow
The world is where the scum settles
worn out

غارقٌ في ا لتوافه  الجُنُون!

\*\*\*

رأيتكِ فانهارَ جسرٌ من اليأسِ
وانفجَرت في جَبينِ الدُّنى
شُرُفاتُ المحبَّة
با لَلفجاءاتِ ثم انكفأتُ بنجوى الطَّعينْ!

\*\*\*

أُحسكِ في غُربةِ الطير
مُرتحلًا في قوافلهِ سادرًا
في ازدحام المَرافيء صخّابةً
أذكر اسمَكِ عبرَ متاهاتِ
وادِي الظنون!

\*\*\*

أعبثُكِ، أحياكِ

54

it drowns in triviality to the point of madness

* * *

I saw you, and the bridge of despair crumbled
On the world's facade
balconies of love erupted
O the wonder of it!
But then I retreated into the unspoken confidences
of a man who has been hurt

* * *

I feel you in the exile of birds
migrating in convoys, reckless
in the clamour of ports
I speak your name across the wilderness
of the valley of suspicion

* * *

You come back to me

في أنَّةِ العطرِ
في زهوةِ الفجرِ
في صَرْخةِ المنحنَى
في تدفُّقِ أمواجٍ كلَّ العُيُونْ!

\* \* \*

أحسُّكَ أعمقَ مما تكنُّ المشاعرُ والذكرياتْ
أقربَ من همسةِ الشكّ للحبِّ
من هزةِ الشوقِ في القلبِ
أنضرَ من فرْحةٍ باليقينْ!

\* \* \*

وأعرفُ أن التَّداني مُحالٌ
وأن اقترابَ المسافاتِ ما بينَنا
قدرٌ مستحيلْ
وأن انبهارَ العُيُون بومْضِ الهَوَى
بَرزخٌ لا يَهُونْ!

\* \* \*

56

in a sigh of perfume
in the splendour of dawn
in the call of a winding road
in the warm goodness flowing from people's eyes

* * *

I feel you deeper than feelings and memories
nearer than a whisper of doubt in the ear of love
than a stir of longing in the heart
more radiant than the joy of certainty

* * *

I know that to be close is impossible
that the narrowing of the distance between us
is unthinkable
and that eyes dazzled by blazing passion
are obstacles that cannot be ignored

* * *

وأعلم أنَّ الزحامَ مُضِلٌّ
وأن المُنى وَجَعٌ مستبدٌّ
وأنكِ عطشى الى النَّهر
والنهرُ معتكِرٌ ثائرٌ
والرمادُ يسربلُ
كلَّ الحُصونْ!

***

دَعيني أخوض في التُّرهاتِ
وحيداً غريباً
ولا تَحفَلي إن رأيتِ المكبَّلَ
يُقتادُ مُرتهناً للمآسي
ويُلقَى بأعماقِ تيهِ السُّجون!

***

سماويَّةٌ أنتِ عُلويَّةٌ
فوق أرض من الطين، والحقدِ، والعُهْر
تُرعِشُها خيلُ كلّ المرابين
فوق مناراتِ عصرِ المُجون!

I know that the crowd are deceivers
and desire is a tyrannical pain
that you thirst for the river
and the river tumbles in muddy fury
and all the fortresses
are heaps of ash

* * *

Let me immerse myself in stupidity
alone, a stranger
Take no notice if you see me in chains
being led as a pawn to disaster
and cast into the labyrinthine depths of prison

* * *

Celestial you are, ethereal
in a land of mud, hate and fornication
shaken by the trampling of money-lenders' horses
over the minarets of the age of debauchery

# في عذاب الصمت

تمرَّدَت الرُّؤى
واصفرَّ وَجهُ اللَّيل
وانتحَبتْ هُنا الجُدْران
وهوَّمَ في ظَلام الغَاب مكتئبٌ
وتاهَ معذَّبٌ حيرانْ
وهأنذا أغنِّي في عَذاب الصَّمْتِ
وَحْدِي أمضغُ الأشْعارْ
وِشاحِي جَمرةً، وعلى جَبيني النَّارْ
وفي جنبيَّ تصطرعُ المُنَى
وتُعَرْبدُ الأشْجانْ
وأركُض في خُطَى الطِّفْل
الذي ركضَتْ به الرَّمضَاءُ
وأهدتْه إلى الأمس المُمزَّق
نَهْلَةُ التِّرياقْ
وَجدتُ الطِّفْلَ
أيَن بشاشةُ الطِّفل الوديع مَضَتْ؟
وكيف خَبَتْ بعينيه مَشَاعِلُ تلْكُمُ الأشواقْ؟

## The Agony of Silence

Dreams rebelled
and the face of night turned pale
even the walls wept here
A melancholy man dozed in the forest gloom
and wandered aimlessly, tormented and distraught
Behold I sing in this agony of silence
alone I stammer out the verses
garlanded with live coals, crowned with fire
desires clash within me
and sorrows run riot
I run in the footsteps of a child
whom the sun-baked ground had spirited away
and given as an antidote
to a tortured yesterday
I found the child
but where were the joyous smiles of that gentle boy?
How had the fires of passion died in his eyes?

وَجدتُ الطِّفلَ

لكنْ بعد ما صَدىء الحنينُ وجفَّتِ الأغْمَاقْ

وجدت الطفلَ

يا للضائعِ المحروم في لُججِ الأسى

تغتالُه الأطواقْ

\*\*\*

حصانُ الفَجرِ ضَاعَ

وغامتِ الذكرى على الشُّطآنْ

وينفضُني الرَّمَادُ

أحس بالموتَى

وبالأكْفَانْ

وفي النهر الملفَّع بالمَرَايَا الحُمْر

أسمعُ صَرخَةَ الحِيتَانْ

وأصغِي للنعيب على الضِّفَافِ السُّمْر

يرفعُ رايةَ الغربانْ

تَضيعُ مَعَ الضَّباب الحَالِكِ الموتُور

تَهْوِي

62

I found the child
but only after the yearning was dulled
    and the depths had run dry
I found the child
poor lost creature
strangled to death
in an abyss of sorrow

* * *

The stallion of dawn has strayed
and memory has faded on the shores
ashes make me tremble
I feel the dead
and their shrouds
and in the river of crimson mirrors
I hear the whales crying out
and listen to the croaking on the dark banks
raising the ravens' standard
Lost in the murky, vengeful fog

قِمَّةُ الانْسَانْ!

***

بعدما انطفأ الحُلْمُ
بعدَ احتباسِ الصَّدَى في الجَنَازَةِ
بعد انتصارِ الكآبة
بعد ما أورقَتْ في صخورِ الأسَى
فوق أطلال كل المروءات
فوقَ الصَّبَاح
ظِلَالُ السَّحَابَة
بعمقُ الجُرْحُ
نتفِضُ المَوْتُ
يبكي على الذِّكْرَيَاتِ
المَسَاء الحَزِينْ
يفرحُ الناعقُون، ينتصِبُ الحاقِدُونَ
يمضونَ كالمَوْج
يمشونَ في موكب الساخِرِينْ
قد يغيبُ الصَّبَاحُ
قد ينبضُ اليَأْسُ
قد يتحدَّى المَنَاراتِ

64

man's dominance

collapses

* * *

After the quenching of the dream

the stifling of the echo in the funeral procession

and the triumph of gloom

after shadows of clouds

have blossomed among rocks of sorrow

and over the ruins of all acts of honour

darkening the morning

the wound grows deeper

death shudders into life

and the sad evening

mourns its memories

The prophets of doom rejoice, the spiteful rise up

and roll by like the waves

in scornful procession

The morning may vanish

the pulse of despair quicken

minarets may be challenged

ينطحُها المارقون
بعدَ أوبته ـ الفجْرِ ـ
يَنحسرُ الظلُّ
يَسقطُ ثوبُ الجَريمةِ في الوَحْلِ
يَنتَحِر المُجْرمونْ!

assaulted by apostates

but when the dawn returns

the shadows will disappear

crime's robe will fall in the mud

and criminals will be their own destroyers

# سياط الذئاب الصفر

تَهَرًّا نايُهُ المَجْرُوحُ
غاضَ الشوقُ من بَحْرِ الرُّؤى
أزرتْ به الشُّطآنُ
وجلَّلَه قَتَامُ الأمسِ
أرَّق فجرَهُ التَّعبُ

*  *  *

يَشُدُّ على خُطاهُ الرَّمل
تَحْصبُهُ رِياحُ التِّيهِ
في وادِي الأَسَى
يَلتذُّ بالجَمَراتِ في بَيْدائِه
يَنْأى، وَيَقْتَربُ

*  *  *

يُجَرِّرُ غُربةَ القَلب المكبَّلِ
مَلَّه وَمْضُ السَّرابِ

## The Scourge of Pale Wolves

His wounded flute is shattered
Desire ebbs from the sea of dreams
The seashores deride him
The gloom of yesterday covers him like a dark shawl
Weariness makes him restless at dawn

* * *

The sand presses on his footsteps
The desert winds spray him with grit and stones
in the valley of sorrows
He delights in the burning embers of the wilderness
draw back, then approach

* * *

He drags along his exiled shackled heart
The glittering mirages have tired of him

يهيمُ فوقَ النَّجْمِ
شَدوُ حياتِه الواحاتُ
لكنْ عمرُهُ لَهَبْ

***

يعيشُ، يعيشُ رَهْنَ الشَّوكِ
رَهْنَ تِلَالِ ماضيه المُضَيَّعِ
في صحارَى الوَهْمِ
تَسْحَقُ حُلْمَهُ
الأمواجُ
والاعْصارُ
والغَضَبْ

***

تَجافَتْهُ البَلابِلُ
فالنَّعيبُ صَدَاهُ
موكِنُهُ الصُّخورُ السُّودُ
حارِسُهُ الضَّبابُ الجَهْمُ

70

He floats over stars
his songs the Oases
in the burning heat of his life

* * *

He lives a hostage to the thorns
to the hills of his wrecked past
in the deserts of illusion
Waves
cyclones
and rage
crush his dream

* * *

Nightingales shun him
and the croaking of ravens fills his ears
His shelter is the black rocks
his guard the sullen fog

مِلْءَ إِنائِهِ
الحِرْمانُ والسَّغَبُ

***

يَقْرَأ في الوجوهِ
صحيفةً رَعْناء
صُورةَ فارغينَ
مُشَوَّهي الأحداقِ والرَّغَبَاتِ
تَرْسُمُ عارَ جيلِ الزَّيْفِ
مِنْ ألْوانِها الصَّخَبُ!

***

يُشَاهِدُ مَسْرَحَ القُطْعَانِ
تحتَ سياطِ نَارِ القَهْرِ
تجلِدُهُ الذِّئابُ الصُّفْرُ
يرقصُ في اللَّهيبِ

His cup is filled with hunger and deprivation

* * *

He reads in the faces around him
a frivolous record of events
an image of empty people
with distorted gazes and warped desires
portraying the shame of a counterfeit generation
in screaming colours

* * *

He watches as herds of beasts
under the fiery whips of coercion
are scourged by pale wolves
In the flames
a moth dances
enraptured

فراشُهُ
طَرَباً، وَيْنْجَذِبُ

\*\*\*

مَتَى يستيقظُ المَأسورُ
مِنْ سَبَحاتِهِ في لُجَّة الأشْجان؟
مَتَى يتبدَّلُ الانسَانُ؟
يْنسى الذلَّ
في فَيْضِ العَطَاء
يضُوعُ، يَنسكِبُ؟!. .

enraptured

* * *

When will the prisoner awake
from his driftings on the ocean of grief?
When will man change
and reject degradation
in a flood of giving
and create and flow forth?

# حقلٌ من النار

لا تَقُلْ في حَقليَ الأعشابُ في حقلكِ نارُ
وَشَرارٌ، وَدَمارُ
والمنادُونَ بإسعافِكَ
قد أعجلَهمْ عنكَ سِفارٌ وفَرارُ
لا تَقلْ في الغَدِ أحلامٌ
فأحلامُكَ غطَّاها الغُبَارُ
والذي تعلِكُهُ الحَصْباءِ والرَّمْلُ المُثَارُ
أنتَ لا يُسنِدُكَ الآلُ قد انهارَ الجِدَارُ
لا تَقُلْ في حَقْلي الأعشابُ
في حَقلكَ نارُ!

## The Field of Fire

Don't say, 'There is grass in my field'
There is fire
and sparks that burn
Those who called out for help on your behalf
have had to desert you and flee
Don't say, 'Tomorrow I will dream dreams'
Your dreams are covered in dust
destroyed by stones and raging sand
You have no kin to support you and the walls
    have all tumbled down
Don't say, 'There is grass in my field'
There is fire

# عندما ينكسر الحلم

أحسُّ الملوحةَ في شفةِ الشمس
ما زال في فمي الملحُ والنار
ما زلتُ حرَّان لم أرتفقْ


***


وما زلتُ أعبر جسرَ المسافات
مُنزلقاً في حوافر خيل الملائك
أسأل مجمرتي حائراً عن مسارِ العبق


***


ونهرُ الشعاع الذي انداح من غرةِ الفجرِ
يغمر دُنيا الكآبة
وانشقَّ من كبدِ الأفق
قد ذابَ

## When the Dream is Broken

I taste the saltiness on the lips of the sun
I still have salt and fire in my mouth
and burn with fruitless passion

* * *

I still cross the bridge that spans the distances
slipping in the hoofprints of angels' horses
I ask my incense-burner in dismay where the
    perfume has gone

* * *

The river of light that flowed from the blaze
    on the forehead of dawn
flooding the gloomy world
that split from the heart of the horizon
has vanished

في ترُّهاتِ الشَّفَق

***

أحسُّ الملوحة
أنسى انتمائيَ لليل
ينحسرُ الحلم
ينكسر السيف في الغمدِ
تعرى البحيرةُ
تسدُّر كلُّ الظنون

***

تُحاصرني أعينُ المتعبينَ الحيارَى
تجلِّلني بقتامِ المآسي الكبار
تجلدني عارياً في النَّهار
ضعيفاً على القيدِ
تسحقني قبضةُ اليأس

80

in the banalities of twilight

* * *

I taste the saltiness
I forget my involvement with the night
the dream vanishes
the sword is broken in the sheath
the lake is stripped bare
and my thoughts are thrown into confusion

* * *

The eyes of the weary and bemused hem me in
wrapping me in the darkness of great calamities
whipping me naked in broad daylight
until I am weak and barely alive
The fist of despair crushes me

يلفظني موكبُ الساخرين!

***

وتجهش في خافقي النارُ
أصرخ ٱلتاع وحدي
أشرُدُ في صخب الغاب وحدي
أمشي على الماء مَشيَ الطعين!

***

رضعناه تيهاً وقهراً
مضغناه جمراً
ولما نزلْ رهن مفترق الغيب
عِشنا ظلال الكآبة
لما يزل طيفُها
سُجُفاً تتحدَّى!

***

the scornful procession casts me aside

* * *

The fire sobs in my heart
I call out, burning with loneliness
wander aimlessly in the tumult of the forest
walk on the water, wounded and alone

* * *

We have drunk the milk of exile and subjugation
chewed on burning coals
and we are still hostages at the crossroads
    of the unknown
We have lived in the shadow of dejection
and its spectre still defies us
an impenetrable veil

* * *

أكادُ، أكادُ أرى

بركاتِ السحائبِ

عطرَ السماواتِ

أشرعةَ الخصبِ

تمضي غُباراً

وترسُمُ لحداً!

***

مَتى يورقُ الصَّخرُ؟

يخضلُّ وادي المروءاتِ بالفجرِ؟

يركض ظلُّ الحدائقِ؟

ينسكبُ الرمْلُ عُشْباً؟

ويندى؟!

84

I can almost see
the grace of the clouds
the fragrance of the skies
the sails of fruitfulness
dwindle into dust
and etch out a grave

\* \* \*

When will the bare rocks burst into leaf
the valley of honour be wet with dew at dawn
shadows race in gardens
and the sand sprout grass
and grow moist and verdant?

# لمن المجد

المجدُ في الحياةِ حَقُّ مشتري الحَيَاة

بكلِّ ما يملكُ بالقُوتِ، وبالفَرْحةِ، بالدَّماء

لَمن يوزِّعُ النَّدَى ويُهرقُ الطُّيُوب

من روحِهِ من قَطَراتِ قلبِه

من وقدةِ العَذَابُ

المجدُ في الحياةِ خالصًا لمن يَمُوتْ

لمبدإٍ، لفكرةٍ، لذرَّةٍ من التُّراب

لصوتِ طَيرٍ هَزِجٍ في أيكةِ الوَطَنْ

لغادةٍ تغسلُ وجهَهَا الدُّموعْ

لبَسمةٍ تلوحُ في محيَّا والدٍ عجوز

للثغةٍ في شفةِ الطِّفل

لضَحكةِ النَّهَرْ

لخيمةٍ تجذبها الرِّياحُ في المَساء

لمُولد النبتةِ في مَطَارف الجبالْ!

## Whose is the Glory?


Glory is the right of him who buys it
with all that he has to eat, with his happiness
   and his blood
the right of him who gives abundantly,
   shedding sweet perfumes
from his soul, from the essence of his heart
from the fires of his suffering
Glory is untarnished for him who would die
for a principle, for an idea, for a speck of dust
for a bird singing from a thicket in his homeland
for a young girl with her face bathed in tears
for an old father's smile
for the faltering words on the lips of a child
for the laughter of a river
for a tent tugged by the evening breeze
for the burgeoning of a green plant on a mountain
   side

# عصبُ الرِّمالْ . . .

| | |
|---|---|
| أَجْراسٌ، يـنـطلِقُ المُـخَـبّـا | الـرّاسُ . . رأسُكَ تصرُخُ الـ |
| زيدٌ أحبَّ ومـا أحـبّ | زُمَـرٌ تَفِحُّ سُـمـومُـهـا |
| ـرَى ناكصاتُ الرّكضِ غَضْبَى | وقـوافِـلٌ تعـدُو وأُخـ |
| لِ ، ومن يُضيعُ العمرَ عَتْبـا | من يَشـتَري عصبَ الـرّمـا |
| ـرُ ذَيْلَه قفـزاً، وعُـجْـبـا | والأغْـرجُ الأعشـى يُجـرِّ |
| ـةِ والفـريسـةُ ليسَ تأْبَى | تَهوي الـذئابُ على الفَـريسـ |
| ـرِ الحُـرِ مَكـرُمَةٍ وخِصْبا | يأَبَى الـرجالُ أذَى الضميـ |
| أَجْـراسٌ ينـطلِقُ المُـخَـبّـا! | والـرّاسُ رأسُكَ تصرُخُ الـ |

88

## The Sinews of the Sands

In your head bells jangle. What is hidden is revealed
Bands of men blow out their poisons. Zayd loves
　　and does not love
Some caravans hurry on their way, others hang back
　　in anger
There are people who buy the sinews of the sands,
　　and those who waste their lives recriminating
The blind cripple drags himself along with a hop
　　of pride
Wolves fall upon their prey and the prey does not
　　resist
Men refuse to harm a free conscience out of honour
　　and generosity of spirit
In your head bells jangle. What is hidden is revealed

# مِن أطيافِ الغَربة

غريبٌ، والدخانُ
وليلُنَا، والسهدُ في الأجفانْ
وأشواقٌ تضجُّ
رُؤى العذابِ تغلُّهَا، تمتصُّهَا
ويَلوكُهَا القُرصانْ
ومَوْجٌ إثر موجٍ
والمصابيحُ الكئيبةُ
والضبابُ يلحُّ، يهزأ بالكهوفِ
ونجمةٌ بلهاءُ
وأشياءُ مخضَّبةٌ، مبعثرةٌ
تُناقضُ روحَها الأشياءُ
وأركُضُ تائهاً
ويُفيقُني من غَشيتِي الطُّوفانْ
وينفضُني الرمادُ على مَرايا الحزنِ
تنتفضُ المَرَايَا
ينتشي من صيْدِهِ الجلَّادُ
ويَضحكُ للضحايا السائرينَ على رَصيفِ الأمسِ

## Some Spectres of Exile

A stranger, and the smoke
and our night, and eyelids heavy with sleeplessness
and tumultuous longings
chained down by visions of suffering, sucked dry
discredited by pirates
wave upon wave
The gloomy street lights
the persistent fog mocking the caves
the dull-witted star
things tinged with other colours, scattered
at odds with their own spirits
I run, distracted
The flood wakes me from my daze
Ashes scatter me on mirrors of sorrow
The mirrors tremble
The hangman exults over his catch
and laughs at his victims as they tread
   yesterday's pavements

فوقَ مِهادِ شوكِ الذلِّ

تحتَ هياكلِ الغربانِ

قد ركَضُوا لغير معَاذْ!

\*\*\*

غريبٌ .. فوقَ أنهارِ المَساءِ

سَرَى بغيرِ شِراعْ

أسيرٌ غاضَ حتَّى القَاعْ

تلوحُ الشمسُ فوقَ وِشاحِه

ترنُو .. وتنغمرُ

يغيبُ سناً

يضيعُ وِشَاحْ

وفي أذنيْه ثرثرةُ الحَيَارى

في ظَلامِ اليَمِّ

تستأني، وتَنحسرُ

ولا نايٌ بكفَّيْه

ولا عودٌ .. ولا وِتَرُ

وفي منفاهُ همهمةُ الرياحِ

92

over thorn beds of humiliation
below temples of ravens
They have run too far to return

* * *

A stranger, he travelled the rivers of evening
without a sail
A prisoner, he sank down to the depths
The sun appears over his bright poet's sash
looks, and then plunges downwards
setting in a blaze of light
The sash is lost
and the sound in his ears of confused chattering
from the murky sea
falters and dies
There is no flute in his fingers
no lute or guitar
only the muttering winds to accompany his
    exile's song

تهزُّهَا الأشباحْ

* * *

غريبٌ يَعلكُ الجَمراتْ
يشدُّ حصانَه لمنابعِ الآلامِ والآهاتِ
تلفظُ ركبَه الساحَاتْ
ويظمأ والسرابُ شَرَابُهُ
وطَعَامهُ الأنّاتْ
يعيشُ وعربداتُ القيظِ تَوْأمُهُ
وجسرُ اليأسِ معبّرُهُ إلى الواحاتْ
أضاعتْه السكينةُ
ضلَّ في شُرُفِ المدينة
مَلَّه الاصّرارُ
مزَّق كُوخَه الاعْصارْ
وغامتْ ملءَ عينيهِ السفُوحُ
وشاهتِ الغاباتْ!

* * *

وأنتِ . . وأنتِ . .

94

driven by shadows

* * *

A stranger, chewing on live coals
he leads his horse to the fountains of sorrows
the city squares reject him
He is thirsty, and drinks the mirage
and feeds on groans
He lives, twin of the riotous heat of high summer
and crosses to oases on a bridge of despair
Tranquillity has passed him by
He has wandered aimlessly on the heights of the city
bored by his own perseverance
The hurricane has torn his hut to pieces
To his jaded eyes the hills are wrapped in cloud
and the forests without beauty

* * *

And you, you

يا هَمْسَ القُرونِ
ودَفقةَ الألحانْ
ذكرتُكِ واعتصرتُ صَدَاكِ
فانفجرتْ بيَ الجُدْرانْ
ذكرتُكِ حالماً بالموتِ، بالمأساةِ
في بَوابةِ الأحْزانْ
ذكرتُك ظامئاً للفجرِ
للأمطارِ
للأصحابِ
مُرتمياً على الشُّطْآنْ
ذكرتُك لَمْ تَزلْ ذِكراك نَهْرا
يغمرُ الأعشابْ
وينقَع غُلَّةَ الغُدْرانْ
ذكرتُك أنتِ يا قَدَر الغريبِ
بساحةِ الحِرمانْ
ويا خيطَ الضياءِ إليَّ
يعبرُ سُدْفةَ الآفاقِ، مُشْتَعِلًا
ويَسْحَبُ حالكَ الأكْفانْ!

\*\*\*

96

O whisper of the centuries

everflowing spring of melody

I remembered you and distilled the echo of your songs

and the walls exploded and let me through

I remembered you, as I dreamed of death and tragedy

in the gateway of sorrows

I remembered you when I thirsted for the dawn

for the rains

for friends

cast up on alien shores

I remembered you. Your memory was forever a river

that flooded the grass

and slaked the burning thirst of the little streams

I remembered you, O destiny of strangers

in the place of deprivation

you were a thread of sheer light for me

perforating the veil of the horizon

and pulling away the dark shrouds

\* \* \*

غريبٌ . . .

غربتي تَعَبٌ . . وإجهاضٌ، وتَرْحَالٌ . .

لغيرِ إيابٍ

غريبٌ . . .

عاشَ ينتظرُ القطارَ

على وصيدِ البابْ!

I am a stranger

My exile is weariness, miscarriage, departure

with no hope of return

a stranger

who has lived waiting for a train

always on the threshold

# رسائل قصيرة

أسيِّدتي
أتيتُكِ في يَدي المِصباحْ
ولا نورٌ
وجُرحُ الأمس ينغُر في تضاعيفي
وهمسٌ منك مخنوقٌ
أكادُ أعيه في حُلْمي
كأنْ هوايَ مشنوقٌ

***

أتيتُكِ لا أخافُ اليأسَ
لا أستنبىءِ الشطآنْ
أتيتُكِ فوق أجنحةٍ
من الآلامِ والحِرمانْ
وكم قد لجَّ في شَفَتي
سؤالٌ مُغلقٌ حيرانْ

## Short Letters

Madam
I came to you with a lamp in my hand
but no light
and the wounds of yesterday burrowing into my heart
You whispered and it was stifled
I almost heard it in my dream
as if my love were strangled

* * *

I came to you not fearing despair
not asking the seashore for news
I came to you on wings of suffering and want
on my lips the same question persisting
confused and obscure

مَتى موعدُنا الآتي ؟

أنا أستثقلُ الوعْدَا

دعيه دعيه للغدِ لا

أرى في يومنا سَعْدا

فلا كوبٌ بأيدينا

ولا زهرُ الرُّبى يشدُو بنا دينا

ولا أنا ذلكَ المفتونْ

وأنتِ الوردةُ السكرَى

عبيرُكِ ضاعَ في الوادي

وخلَّفَ لوْعةً مرَّة

لقلبي النائحِ الشادي

دعي العِطْرا

وخلِّي النهرَ يركضُ شبةَ مذعورٍ

فلا شدْوُ الشحارير

ولا سِحرُ التصاوير

يعيدُ لنا جَنى العمرِ

ويسكبُ شعلةَ النور

'When will we meet again?'
I find it hard to make promises
Leave it till tomorrow
I see no good fortune today
no glasses of joy in our hands
no wild flowers singing holy songs to us
nor am I that enchanted lover
nor are you that drunken rose
Your fragrance was wasted in the valley
leaving bitter anguish behind
in my weeping singing heart
Forget the perfume
and let the river run on half-scared
Neither the singing of the blackbirds
nor the magic of changing scenes
can bring back our lives' rich harvest
and rekindle the blaze of light

أسيّدتي
معطَّلةٌ برامجُنا
مضيَّعةٌ على الدرْبِ
ومنذُ ربيعِنا الثاني
ومنذُ خنقتُ بين يديكِ نَيْساني
ومنذُ ركضتِ تكتشفينَ
فيٌّ منابعَ الأمسِ
نفتُّ في دمي الليلُ
وخدَّر طاقتي الويلُ
فلا الأوتارُ لا الألحانُ تدعوني
ولا أنا من عرفتِ ، وأنتِ من أنتِ ؟
كلانا سائرٌ في درْب ماضيه
كلانا يرتَوي ـ مُتَرنِّحاً ـ من منهلِ التيهِ
بعبّى؛ موكبَ الذكرى
لحفْلٍ في لياليه
يُلوِّن وهْمَه يُلقي عليه وشاحْ
وعِطرَ أقاحْ
ولكن تفضُح المرآةُ سُهْداً في مآقيهِ!

Our plans have come to naught

lost on the road

and since our second springtime

since I strangled the month of April before your eyes

since you rushed to discover

yesterday's fountains in me

the night in my blood has crumbled away

and woe has blunted my powers

Stringed instruments playing sweet melodies

     no longer call to me

I am not the man you knew, and you, who are you?

both of us are travelling the roads of our

     separate pasts

Both of us drunkenly quenching our thirst at the

     spring of distraction

lining up the parade of memories

for future nights

dressing up our illusions with garlands and ribbons

drowning them in the scent of chrysanthemums

but the mirror exposes the sleeplessness in the

     corners of our eyes

أسيّدتي

أنا الشاكي

سكبتُ هنا ضَرَاعاتي

وحين طرقتُ بابَ الفجرِ لم يأبَهْ لمأساتي

وقهقه ساخراً كالذئبِ

في أُذني

وعدتُ لسجنِ شبّاكي

أنا الشاكي

أسيّدتي

جدارُ العزلةِ الحمراءِ

أثقبُه بأظفاري

أجرجرُ في دروبِ الليلِ أحلامي

وأنثُر فيه أزهاري

وأقرأُ قِصَّتي وحدي

على وَهْجٍ من النارِ

–3–

Madam

I am the one with a grievance

I have poured out my entreaties here

and when I knocked at the door of the morning

   it paid no heed to my suffering

and snorted mocking wolfish laughter

in my ears

and I went back to the prison of my window

I am the one with a grievance


–4–

Madam

In the wall of crimson solitude

I scratch a hole with my nails

I trail my dreams behind me on the roads of night

and strew the way with flowers

I read my story alone

by the fire's glow

حكايةَ متعبٍ

قد عاشَ بين الظفرِ والنابِ

وحيداً جِدَّ مرتابِ

فتاتُ موائدي

قد عادَ لي زادي وترياقي

وكم من قطَّةٍ ماءت

على قَدَمي

وكم قلبي أراقَ دمي

زكيّاً فوقَ أوراقي

ولكن ليسَ من يصغي لأشعاري

ولا من زائرٍ داري

جدارُ العزلةِ الحمراء

أثقبُهُ بأظفاري!

the story of a weary man
who lived between the devil and the deep blue sea
alone and full of doubts
The crumbs from my table
became my food, my antidote
Innumerable cats came mewing
at my feet
More times than I remember I shed my heart's blood
unmixed on the paper where I wrote
But there's no one to listen to my verses
no one to visit my house
In the wall of crimson solitude
I scratch a hole with my nails

# صورة

رأيت في مخدعها المعطَّر
صورةَ زوجٍ أشيبٍ قد ماتَ منذ أشهرِ
دموعُها كالمطرِ
عليه تذريها طفل الصائدِ المغرِّرِ
تقولُ كان عدَّتي
وكان زادَ سفَري
كان يقيني من زمانٍ أكدرِ
ذكراه في قلبي تموجُ
كالدَّمِ
وصوتُه، سعلته في مِسمَعي
كالنغمِ
أصداؤه تَملأ داري
عطفهُ كالنَّهَرِ
لكنني أنا سئمتُ ضجري
فاسطع بواديَّ إذا
شئتَ سطوعَ القَمَرِ


\*\*\*

110

## A Picture

I saw in her perfumed chamber
a picture of her husband, an old man who'd died
    some months before
Her tears fell like rain
She cried over him like a frustrated child, as if
    he'd run away from her
She said, 'He was all I needed
the provisions for my journey
the one I could be sure of in the bad times
His memory surges through my heart like blood
his voice, his cough
had their own melody for me
their echoes fill my home
his tenderness was like a river
But I have grown bored with my own unhappiness
so shine in my valley, if you want to
like the full moon.'

\* \* \*

111

وبعد شهرٍ حوَّمتْ تسألني

يا حلميَ العزيز

هل تغارُ منه ؟ من ماضٍ معي ؟

وقفتُه عليه فهو جذوةٌ في أضلُعي ؟

فلم أقلْ شيئاً لها

لكنني قبَّلتُها، عصرتُها

حطَّمتُها في نَهَمٍ

وصورةُ الأشيب ترنو لي بعينيْ ضيغمٍ

كمارِدٍ في قمقمٍ

تهزُّني من حلمي

لكنني لم أرتعشْ، لم أكترثْ

لكنني لم أندم

فقد رأيتُ في عناقِها الظَّمِي

كلَّ كيانٍ عمرِها بي يحتمي

112

After a month, she hovered round me, asking me

'Dear heart

are you jealous of him

of his past with me

of the time I devoted just to him

when he was a burning fire in my side?'

I said nothing

but I kissed her, squeezed her

crushed her to me in greedy passion

and the old man gazed at me from his picture

with the eyes of a lion

like a genie in a bottle

shaking me out of my dream

But I wasn't shaken

I didn't care

I had no regrets

For I'd seen

in her hungry embrace

her whole being

take refuge in me

Me jealous? Not likely!

أغارُ ويحي ؟ ٱلغارُ من صدّى مهدَّمِ ؟

\*\*\*

تَوارتِ الصورةُ بعد أشهرِ
ونسخ الحاضرُ كلَّ الأسطرِ . . . !

Jealous of a shattered echo?

* * *

In a few months the picture was gone
The past cancelled out by the present

# همسة

وكيف بهَمسةٍ مذعورةٍ وبنظرةٍ عجْلَى

أسرْتِ الخافقَ المسحورَ . . . ما رَاءى وما استعلى

هَفا كالطيْرِ نحوَكِ

كالوليدِ لأمّهِ يحبُو

كَسرْبِ الزهرِ في نَيْسانَ كالسُّحُبِ الربيعيَّة

كأمطارِ الخريفِ إذا تصَبَّت روضةً عَطشى

كموْجِ المدَّ خجلانا يدبُّ لأرجلٍ كسلى

***

نِصالُ الغدرِ أورثْ خافِقي دهراً

سقتْهُ المرَّ في كأسٍ من الأحزانِ لا تَبلى

وجرَّحَهُ صِراعُ الهجرِ بينَ الوصلِ والحِرْمان

تَعاصَى خافِقي . . . هَرمَ الفؤادُ

نكيفَ شَدَّته ؟

إلى ظلِّ الهَوَى عينان

## A Whisper

How did you capture my heart for ever
with a timid whisper and a swift glance?
It fluttered towards you like a bird
like a child, creeping close to his mother
You made the April flowers burst open like
    clouds in springtime
You were like autumn rains drenching a thirsty
    meadow
like the waves of high tide shyly lapping
    round indolent feet

* * *

The knives of treachery have seared my heart
    for an eternity
given it myrrh to drink in a bottomless cup of sorrows
The conflict of parting, between having and not
    having love, has wounded it
it has grown old and obstinate
So how did two eyes draw it into passion's shadow

وأوغَلَ في الشغافِ رسيسُ حُبٍّ واستفاقَ حَنانْ

سَلي عينيكِ عن قَلبى

سليها يا طفولَةَ حُلمىَ النشوانْ

ففي عينيكِ من ماضىً أشواقُ الغدِ الحَيْرى

وفي عينيكِ جُرْحُ الأمسِ . . . أمسى باهتاً مترنِّحَ الألوانْ!

***

هجرتُ الحبَّ . . . سَوْطُ اليأسِ يجرفُ فرحةَ المُشْتاقْ

شِباكُ الحبِّ كم مرَّ الهَوَى منهنَّ

كم أفنَيتِ . . . كم أقصَيتِ طيفَ حِسّانْ

وها قد جاء طَيفُكِ مارداً لا يرهَبُ الجُدْرانْ

برغمىَ . . . هزَّني سِحْرٌ بعينِك يعصِبُ الآلامْ

ويفتحُ كوَّةَ الشوقِ الحبيسِ

ويطلقُ الألحانْ !!

118

and a patina of love form round it as
   tenderness revived?
Ask your eyes about my heart
Ask them, child of my rapturous dream
for in your eyes are the confused longings of
   tomorrow rising from my past
and the wounds of yesterday grown pale,
   their colours quivering


* * *


I fled from love. The whip of despair drove out the
   joy of longing
Passion slipped through the nets of love so many times
and I escaped. I chased away visions of
   beautiful women
and then the vision of you appeared, defiant,
   undaunted by high walls
In spite of myself I was stirred by the magic in
   your eyes, muffling pain
Letting out my stifled longing
and setting sweet melodies free